ADDRESS BOOK
ELEPHANT

The Pocket Size Address Book

All rights reserved. No part of this document may be reproduced or transmitted in any form or by any means, electronic or otherwise. This means that you cannot record or photocopy any material Ideas, tips or suggestions that are provided in this book

www.journalsrus.com

Address Book Elephant
© 2016 Ciparum LLC
All rights reserved.
ISBN-10:1-63589-047-0
ISBN-13:978-1-63589-047-1

Table of Content

Name	Page	Name	Page
John Doe	24		

Name	Page	Name	Page

Name	Page	Name	Page

THIS PAGE WAS
INTENTIONALLY
LEFT BLANK

NAME..
ADDRESS..
....
MOBILE # (Cell)..
HOME #...
WORK #...
FAX...
EMAIL...

NAME..
ADDRESS..
....
MOBILE # (Cell)..
HOME #...
WORK #...
FAX...
EMAIL...

NAME..
ADDRESS..
....
MOBILE # (Cell)..
HOME #...
WORK #...
FAX...
EMAIL...

NOTES:

NAME...
ADDRESS..
....
MOBILE # (Cell)...
HOME #..
WORK #..
FAX..
EMAIL...

NAME...
ADDRESS..
....
MOBILE # (Cell)...
HOME #..
WORK #..
FAX..
EMAIL...

NAME...
ADDRESS..
....
MOBILE # (Cell)...
HOME #..
WORK #..
FAX..
EMAIL...

NOTES:

NAME..
ADDRESS..
....
MOBILE # (Cell)..
HOME #...
WORK #...
FAX..
EMAIL...

NAME..
ADDRESS..
....
MOBILE # (Cell)..
HOME #...
WORK #...
FAX..
EMAIL...

NAME..
ADDRESS..
....
MOBILE # (Cell)..
HOME #...
WORK #...
FAX..
EMAIL...

NOTES:

NAME..
ADDRESS...
....
MOBILE # (Cell)...
HOME #...
WORK #...
FAX..
EMAIL...

NAME..
ADDRESS...
....
MOBILE # (Cell)...
HOME #...
WORK #...
FAX..
EMAIL...

NAME..
ADDRESS...
....
MOBILE # (Cell)...
HOME #...
WORK #...
FAX..
EMAIL...

NOTES:

NAME..
ADDRESS...
....
MOBILE # (Cell)...
HOME #...
WORK #...
FAX..
EMAIL...

NAME..
ADDRESS...
....
MOBILE # (Cell)...
HOME #...
WORK #...
FAX..
EMAIL...

NAME..
ADDRESS...
....
MOBILE # (Cell)...
HOME #...
WORK #...
FAX..
EMAIL...

NOTES:

NAME..
ADDRESS..
....
MOBILE # (Cell)..
HOME #..
WORK #..
FAX..
EMAIL..

NAME..
ADDRESS..
....
MOBILE # (Cell)..
HOME #..
WORK #..
FAX..
EMAIL..

NAME..
ADDRESS..
....
MOBILE # (Cell)..
HOME #..
WORK #..
FAX..
EMAIL..

NOTES:

NAME..
ADDRESS..
....
MOBILE # (Cell)..
HOME #...
WORK #...
FAX...
EMAIL...

NAME..
ADDRESS..
....
MOBILE # (Cell)..
HOME #...
WORK #...
FAX...
EMAIL...

NAME..
ADDRESS..
....
MOBILE # (Cell)..
HOME #...
WORK #...
FAX...
EMAIL...

NOTES:

NAME..
ADDRESS..
....
MOBILE # (Cell)...
HOME #..
WORK #..
FAX...
EMAIL..

NAME..
ADDRESS..
....
MOBILE # (Cell)...
HOME #..
WORK #..
FAX...
EMAIL..

NAME..
ADDRESS..
....
MOBILE # (Cell)...
HOME #..
WORK #..
FAX...
EMAIL..

NOTES:

NAME..
ADDRESS...
....
MOBILE # (Cell)..
HOME #..
WORK #..
FAX...
EMAIL...

NAME..
ADDRESS...
....
MOBILE # (Cell)..
HOME #..
WORK #..
FAX...
EMAIL...

NAME..
ADDRESS...
....
MOBILE # (Cell)..
HOME #..
WORK #..
FAX...
EMAIL...

NOTES:

NAME..
ADDRESS..
....
MOBILE # (Cell)...
HOME #...
WORK #..
FAX...
EMAIL..

NAME..
ADDRESS..
....
MOBILE # (Cell)...
HOME #...
WORK #..
FAX...
EMAIL..

NAME..
ADDRESS..
....
MOBILE # (Cell)...
HOME #...
WORK #..
FAX...
EMAIL..

NOTES:

NAME..
ADDRESS..
....
MOBILE # (Cell)..
HOME #...
WORK #...
FAX..
EMAIL...

NAME..
ADDRESS..
....
MOBILE # (Cell)..
HOME #...
WORK #...
FAX..
EMAIL...

NAME..
ADDRESS..
....
MOBILE # (Cell)..
HOME #...
WORK #...
FAX..
EMAIL...

NOTES:

NAME..
ADDRESS..
....
MOBILE # (Cell)..
HOME #..
WORK #..
FAX...
EMAIL...

NAME..
ADDRESS..
....
MOBILE # (Cell)..
HOME #..
WORK #..
FAX...
EMAIL...

NAME..
ADDRESS..
....
MOBILE # (Cell)..
HOME #..
WORK #..
FAX...
EMAIL...

NOTES:

NAME..
ADDRESS...
....
MOBILE # (Cell)..
HOME #...
WORK #...
FAX..
EMAIL...

NAME..
ADDRESS...
....
MOBILE # (Cell)..
HOME #...
WORK #...
FAX..
EMAIL...

NAME..
ADDRESS...
....
MOBILE # (Cell)..
HOME #...
WORK #...
FAX..
EMAIL...

NOTES:

NAME..
ADDRESS...
....
MOBILE # (Cell)..
HOME #...
WORK #...
FAX..
EMAIL..

NAME..
ADDRESS...
....
MOBILE # (Cell)..
HOME #...
WORK #...
FAX..
EMAIL..

NAME..
ADDRESS...
....
MOBILE # (Cell)..
HOME #...
WORK #...
FAX..
EMAIL..

NOTES:

NAME...
ADDRESS..
....
MOBILE # (Cell)..
HOME #..
WORK #..
FAX..
EMAIL..

NAME...
ADDRESS..
....
MOBILE # (Cell)..
HOME #..
WORK #..
FAX..
EMAIL..

NAME...
ADDRESS..
....
MOBILE # (Cell)..
HOME #..
WORK #..
FAX..
EMAIL..

NOTES:

NAME..
ADDRESS...
....
MOBILE # (Cell)..
HOME #...
WORK #...
FAX...
EMAIL..

NAME..
ADDRESS...
....
MOBILE # (Cell)..
HOME #...
WORK #...
FAX...
EMAIL..

NAME..
ADDRESS...
....
MOBILE # (Cell)..
HOME #...
WORK #...
FAX...
EMAIL..

NOTES:

NAME..
ADDRESS..
....
MOBILE # (Cell)...
HOME #..
WORK #..
FAX...
EMAIL..

NAME..
ADDRESS..
....
MOBILE # (Cell)...
HOME #..
WORK #..
FAX...
EMAIL..

NAME..
ADDRESS..
....
MOBILE # (Cell)...
HOME #..
WORK #..
FAX...
EMAIL..

NOTES:

NAME..
ADDRESS..
....
MOBILE # (Cell)...
HOME #...
WORK #..
FAX..
EMAIL...

NAME..
ADDRESS..
....
MOBILE # (Cell)...
HOME #...
WORK #..
FAX..
EMAIL...

NAME..
ADDRESS..
....
MOBILE # (Cell)...
HOME #...
WORK #..
FAX..
EMAIL...

NOTES:

NAME..
ADDRESS..
....
MOBILE # (Cell)...
HOME #..
WORK #...
FAX..
EMAIL..

NAME..
ADDRESS..
....
MOBILE # (Cell)...
HOME #..
WORK #...
FAX..
EMAIL..

NAME..
ADDRESS..
....
MOBILE # (Cell)...
HOME #..
WORK #...
FAX..
EMAIL..

NOTES:

NAME..
ADDRESS..
....
MOBILE # (Cell)...
HOME #...
WORK #...
FAX..
EMAIL...

NAME..
ADDRESS..
....
MOBILE # (Cell)...
HOME #...
WORK #...
FAX..
EMAIL...

NAME..
ADDRESS..
....
MOBILE # (Cell)...
HOME #...
WORK #...
FAX..
EMAIL...

NOTES:

NAME..
ADDRESS..
....
MOBILE # (Cell)...
HOME #..
WORK #...
FAX...
EMAIL..

NAME..
ADDRESS..
....
MOBILE # (Cell)...
HOME #..
WORK #...
FAX...
EMAIL..

NAME..
ADDRESS..
....
MOBILE # (Cell)...
HOME #..
WORK #...
FAX...
EMAIL..

NOTES:

NAME..
ADDRESS...
....
MOBILE # (Cell)...
HOME #...
WORK #..
FAX..
EMAIL...

NAME..
ADDRESS...
....
MOBILE # (Cell)...
HOME #...
WORK #..
FAX..
EMAIL...

NAME..
ADDRESS...
....
MOBILE # (Cell)...
HOME #...
WORK #..
FAX..
EMAIL...

NOTES:

NAME..
ADDRESS..
....
MOBILE # (Cell)..
HOME #...
WORK #...
FAX...
EMAIL..

NAME..
ADDRESS..
....
MOBILE # (Cell)..
HOME #...
WORK #...
FAX...
EMAIL..

NAME..
ADDRESS..
....
MOBILE # (Cell)..
HOME #...
WORK #...
FAX...
EMAIL..

NOTES:

NAME..
ADDRESS..
....
MOBILE # (Cell)..
HOME #..
WORK #..
FAX...
EMAIL..

NAME..
ADDRESS..
....
MOBILE # (Cell)..
HOME #..
WORK #..
FAX...
EMAIL..

NAME..
ADDRESS..
....
MOBILE # (Cell)..
HOME #..
WORK #..
FAX...
EMAIL..

NOTES:

NAME..
ADDRESS..
....
MOBILE # (Cell)...
HOME #..
WORK #..
FAX...
EMAIL...

NAME..
ADDRESS..
....
MOBILE # (Cell)...
HOME #..
WORK #..
FAX...
EMAIL...

NAME..
ADDRESS..
....
MOBILE # (Cell)...
HOME #..
WORK #..
FAX...
EMAIL...

NOTES:

NAME..
ADDRESS..
....
MOBILE # (Cell)...
HOME #..
WORK #..
FAX...
EMAIL...

NAME..
ADDRESS..
....
MOBILE # (Cell)...
HOME #..
WORK #..
FAX...
EMAIL...

NAME..
ADDRESS..
....
MOBILE # (Cell)...
HOME #..
WORK #..
FAX...
EMAIL...

NOTES:

NAME..
ADDRESS...
....
MOBILE # (Cell)...
HOME #..
WORK #...
FAX...
EMAIL..

NAME..
ADDRESS...
....
MOBILE # (Cell)...
HOME #..
WORK #...
FAX...
EMAIL..

NAME..
ADDRESS...
....
MOBILE # (Cell)...
HOME #..
WORK #...
FAX...
EMAIL..

NOTES:

NAME..
ADDRESS..
....
MOBILE # (Cell)..
HOME #..
WORK #..
FAX..
EMAIL..

NAME..
ADDRESS..
....
MOBILE # (Cell)..
HOME #..
WORK #..
FAX..
EMAIL..

NAME..
ADDRESS..
....
MOBILE # (Cell)..
HOME #..
WORK #..
FAX..
EMAIL..

NOTES:

NAME..
ADDRESS..
....
MOBILE # (Cell)...
HOME #...
WORK #...
FAX..
EMAIL..

NAME..
ADDRESS..
....
MOBILE # (Cell)...
HOME #...
WORK #...
FAX..
EMAIL..

NAME..
ADDRESS..
....
MOBILE # (Cell)...
HOME #...
WORK #...
FAX..
EMAIL..

NOTES:

NAME..
ADDRESS..
....
MOBILE # (Cell)..
HOME #..
WORK #...
FAX..
EMAIL..

NAME..
ADDRESS..
....
MOBILE # (Cell)..
HOME #..
WORK #...
FAX..
EMAIL..

NAME..
ADDRESS..
....
MOBILE # (Cell)..
HOME #..
WORK #...
FAX..
EMAIL..

NOTES:

NAME..
ADDRESS..
....
MOBILE # (Cell)..
HOME #...
WORK #...
FAX..
EMAIL..

NAME..
ADDRESS..
....
MOBILE # (Cell)..
HOME #...
WORK #...
FAX..
EMAIL..

NAME..
ADDRESS..
....
MOBILE # (Cell)..
HOME #...
WORK #...
FAX..
EMAIL..

NOTES:

NAME..
ADDRESS..
....
MOBILE # (Cell)...
HOME #..
WORK #..
FAX...
EMAIL...

NAME..
ADDRESS..
....
MOBILE # (Cell)...
HOME #..
WORK #..
FAX...
EMAIL...

NAME..
ADDRESS..
....
MOBILE # (Cell)...
HOME #..
WORK #..
FAX...
EMAIL...

NOTES:

NAME..
ADDRESS..
....
MOBILE # (Cell)..
HOME #...
WORK #..
FAX..
EMAIL...

NAME..
ADDRESS..
....
MOBILE # (Cell)..
HOME #...
WORK #..
FAX..
EMAIL...

NAME..
ADDRESS..
....
MOBILE # (Cell)..
HOME #...
WORK #..
FAX..
EMAIL...

NOTES:

NAME..
ADDRESS..
....
MOBILE # (Cell)...
HOME #...
WORK #...
FAX..
EMAIL..

NAME..
ADDRESS..
....
MOBILE # (Cell)...
HOME #...
WORK #...
FAX..
EMAIL..

NAME..
ADDRESS..
....
MOBILE # (Cell)...
HOME #...
WORK #...
FAX..
EMAIL..

NOTES:

NAME..
ADDRESS..
....
MOBILE # (Cell)..
HOME #..
WORK #...
FAX...
EMAIL..

NAME..
ADDRESS..
....
MOBILE # (Cell)..
HOME #..
WORK #...
FAX...
EMAIL..

NAME..
ADDRESS..
....
MOBILE # (Cell)..
HOME #..
WORK #...
FAX...
EMAIL..

NOTES:

NAME..
ADDRESS..
....
MOBILE # (Cell)...
HOME #...
WORK #..
FAX..
EMAIL..

NAME..
ADDRESS..
....
MOBILE # (Cell)...
HOME #...
WORK #..
FAX..
EMAIL..

NAME..
ADDRESS..
....
MOBILE # (Cell)...
HOME #...
WORK #..
FAX..
EMAIL..

NOTES:

NAME..
ADDRESS..
....
MOBILE # (Cell)..
HOME #..
WORK #..
FAX...
EMAIL..

NAME..
ADDRESS..
....
MOBILE # (Cell)..
HOME #..
WORK #..
FAX...
EMAIL..

NAME..
ADDRESS..
....
MOBILE # (Cell)..
HOME #..
WORK #..
FAX...
EMAIL..

NOTES:

NAME..
ADDRESS..
....
MOBILE # (Cell)..
HOME #...
WORK #...
FAX..
EMAIL..

NAME..
ADDRESS..
....
MOBILE # (Cell)..
HOME #...
WORK #...
FAX..
EMAIL..

NAME..
ADDRESS..
....
MOBILE # (Cell)..
HOME #...
WORK #...
FAX..
EMAIL..

NOTES:

NAME..
ADDRESS..
....
MOBILE # (Cell)...
HOME #..
WORK #..
FAX...
EMAIL...

NAME..
ADDRESS..
....
MOBILE # (Cell)...
HOME #..
WORK #..
FAX...
EMAIL...

NAME..
ADDRESS..
....
MOBILE # (Cell)...
HOME #..
WORK #..
FAX...
EMAIL...

NOTES:

NAME..
ADDRESS..
....
MOBILE # (Cell)..
HOME #..
WORK #...
FAX..
EMAIL..

NAME..
ADDRESS..
....
MOBILE # (Cell)..
HOME #..
WORK #...
FAX..
EMAIL..

NAME..
ADDRESS..
....
MOBILE # (Cell)..
HOME #..
WORK #...
FAX..
EMAIL..

NOTES:

NAME..
ADDRESS..
....
MOBILE # (Cell)..
HOME #...
WORK #..
FAX..
EMAIL...

NAME..
ADDRESS..
....
MOBILE # (Cell)..
HOME #...
WORK #..
FAX..
EMAIL...

NAME..
ADDRESS..
....
MOBILE # (Cell)..
HOME #...
WORK #..
FAX..
EMAIL...

NOTES:

NAME..
ADDRESS..
....
MOBILE # (Cell)...
HOME #..
WORK #...
FAX...
EMAIL..

NAME..
ADDRESS..
....
MOBILE # (Cell)...
HOME #..
WORK #...
FAX...
EMAIL..

NAME..
ADDRESS..
....
MOBILE # (Cell)...
HOME #..
WORK #...
FAX...
EMAIL..

NOTES:

NAME..
ADDRESS..
....
MOBILE # (Cell)..
HOME #...
WORK #...
FAX...
EMAIL...

NAME..
ADDRESS..
....
MOBILE # (Cell)..
HOME #...
WORK #...
FAX...
EMAIL...

NAME..
ADDRESS..
....
MOBILE # (Cell)..
HOME #...
WORK #...
FAX...
EMAIL...

NOTES:

NAME..
ADDRESS...
....
MOBILE # (Cell)...
HOME #...
WORK #...
FAX...
EMAIL..

NAME..
ADDRESS...
....
MOBILE # (Cell)...
HOME #...
WORK #...
FAX...
EMAIL..

NAME..
ADDRESS...
....
MOBILE # (Cell)...
HOME #...
WORK #...
FAX...
EMAIL..

NOTES:

NAME..
ADDRESS..
....
MOBILE # (Cell)...
HOME #...
WORK #..
FAX..
EMAIL..

NAME..
ADDRESS..
....
MOBILE # (Cell)...
HOME #...
WORK #..
FAX..
EMAIL..

NAME..
ADDRESS..
....
MOBILE # (Cell)...
HOME #...
WORK #..
FAX..
EMAIL..

NOTES:

NAME..
ADDRESS..
....
MOBILE # (Cell)..
HOME #..
WORK #..
FAX...
EMAIL...

NAME..
ADDRESS..
....
MOBILE # (Cell)..
HOME #..
WORK #..
FAX...
EMAIL...

NAME..
ADDRESS..
....
MOBILE # (Cell)..
HOME #..
WORK #..
FAX...
EMAIL...

NOTES:

NAME..
ADDRESS..
....
MOBILE # (Cell)...
HOME #..
WORK #..
FAX..
EMAIL...

NAME..
ADDRESS..
....
MOBILE # (Cell)...
HOME #..
WORK #..
FAX..
EMAIL...

NAME..
ADDRESS..
....
MOBILE # (Cell)...
HOME #..
WORK #..
FAX..
EMAIL...

NOTES:

NAME..
ADDRESS...
....
MOBILE # (Cell)...
HOME #..
WORK #...
FAX..
EMAIL...

NAME..
ADDRESS...
....
MOBILE # (Cell)...
HOME #..
WORK #...
FAX..
EMAIL...

NAME..
ADDRESS...
....
MOBILE # (Cell)...
HOME #..
WORK #...
FAX..
EMAIL...

NOTES:

NAME..
ADDRESS...
....
MOBILE # (Cell)..
HOME #...
WORK #...
FAX..
EMAIL..

NAME..
ADDRESS...
....
MOBILE # (Cell)..
HOME #...
WORK #...
FAX..
EMAIL..

NAME..
ADDRESS...
....
MOBILE # (Cell)..
HOME #...
WORK #...
FAX..
EMAIL..

NOTES:

NAME..
ADDRESS..
....
MOBILE # (Cell)...
HOME #..
WORK #...
FAX..
EMAIL..

NAME..
ADDRESS..
....
MOBILE # (Cell)...
HOME #..
WORK #...
FAX..
EMAIL..

NAME..
ADDRESS..
....
MOBILE # (Cell)...
HOME #..
WORK #...
FAX..
EMAIL..

NOTES:

NAME..
ADDRESS..
....
MOBILE # (Cell)..
HOME #...
WORK #...
FAX...
EMAIL..

NAME..
ADDRESS..
....
MOBILE # (Cell)..
HOME #...
WORK #...
FAX...
EMAIL..

NAME..
ADDRESS..
....
MOBILE # (Cell)..
HOME #...
WORK #...
FAX...
EMAIL..

NOTES:

NAME..
ADDRESS..
....
MOBILE # (Cell)..
HOME #...
WORK #..
FAX..
EMAIL..

NAME..
ADDRESS..
....
MOBILE # (Cell)..
HOME #...
WORK #..
FAX..
EMAIL..

NAME..
ADDRESS..
....
MOBILE # (Cell)..
HOME #...
WORK #..
FAX..
EMAIL..

NOTES:

NAME..
ADDRESS...
....
MOBILE # (Cell)...
HOME #..
WORK #..
FAX..
EMAIL...

NAME..
ADDRESS...
....
MOBILE # (Cell)...
HOME #..
WORK #..
FAX..
EMAIL...

NAME..
ADDRESS...
....
MOBILE # (Cell)...
HOME #..
WORK #..
FAX..
EMAIL...

NOTES:

NAME..
ADDRESS..
....
MOBILE # (Cell)..
HOME #..
WORK #..
FAX...
EMAIL..

NAME..
ADDRESS..
....
MOBILE # (Cell)..
HOME #..
WORK #..
FAX...
EMAIL..

NAME..
ADDRESS..
....
MOBILE # (Cell)..
HOME #..
WORK #..
FAX...
EMAIL..

NOTES:

NAME..
ADDRESS..
....
MOBILE # (Cell)...
HOME #...
WORK #..
FAX..
EMAIL...

NAME..
ADDRESS..
....
MOBILE # (Cell)...
HOME #...
WORK #..
FAX..
EMAIL...

NAME..
ADDRESS..
....
MOBILE # (Cell)...
HOME #...
WORK #..
FAX..
EMAIL...

NOTES:

www.ingramcontent.com/pod-product-compliance
Lightning Source LLC
Chambersburg PA
CBHW052118070526
44584CB00017B/2545